Watch & Learn

Sign Language for Beginners

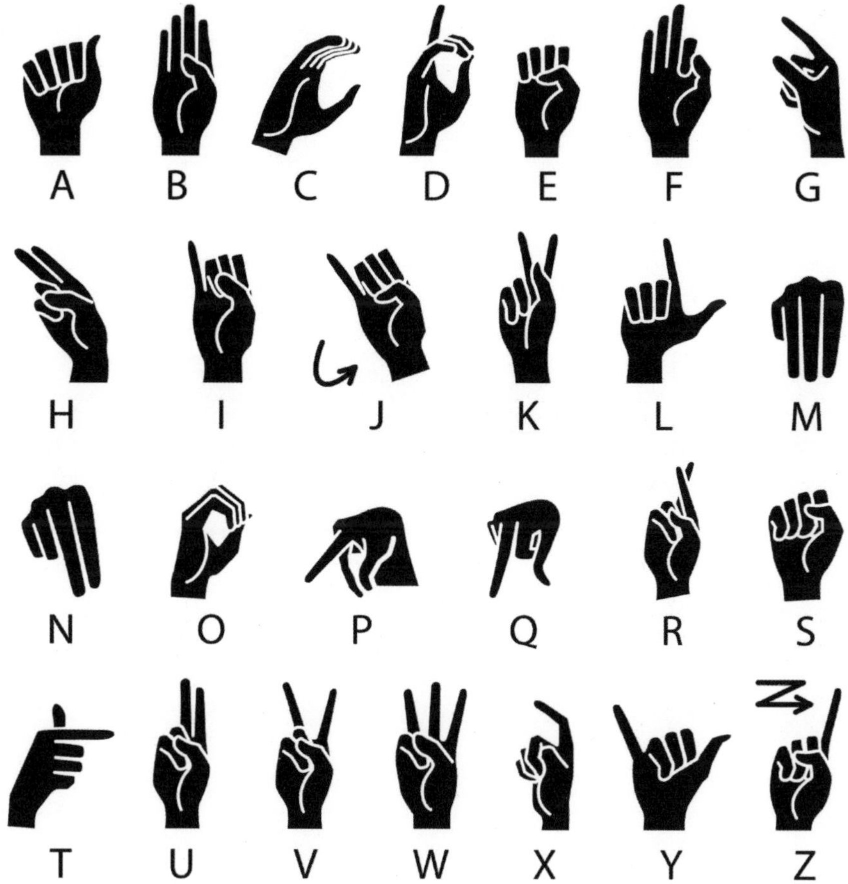

Sushil Thind

First published in paperback by
Michael Terence Publishing in 2019
www.mtp.agency

ISBN 9781913289690

Michael Terence
Publishing

Aa

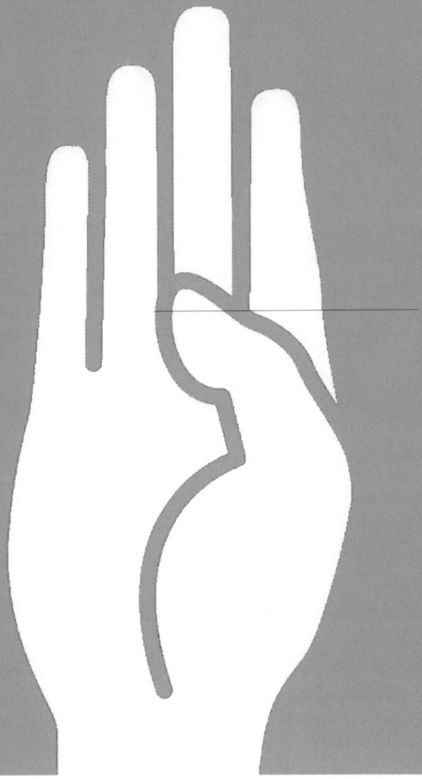

Bb

Cc

Dd

Ee

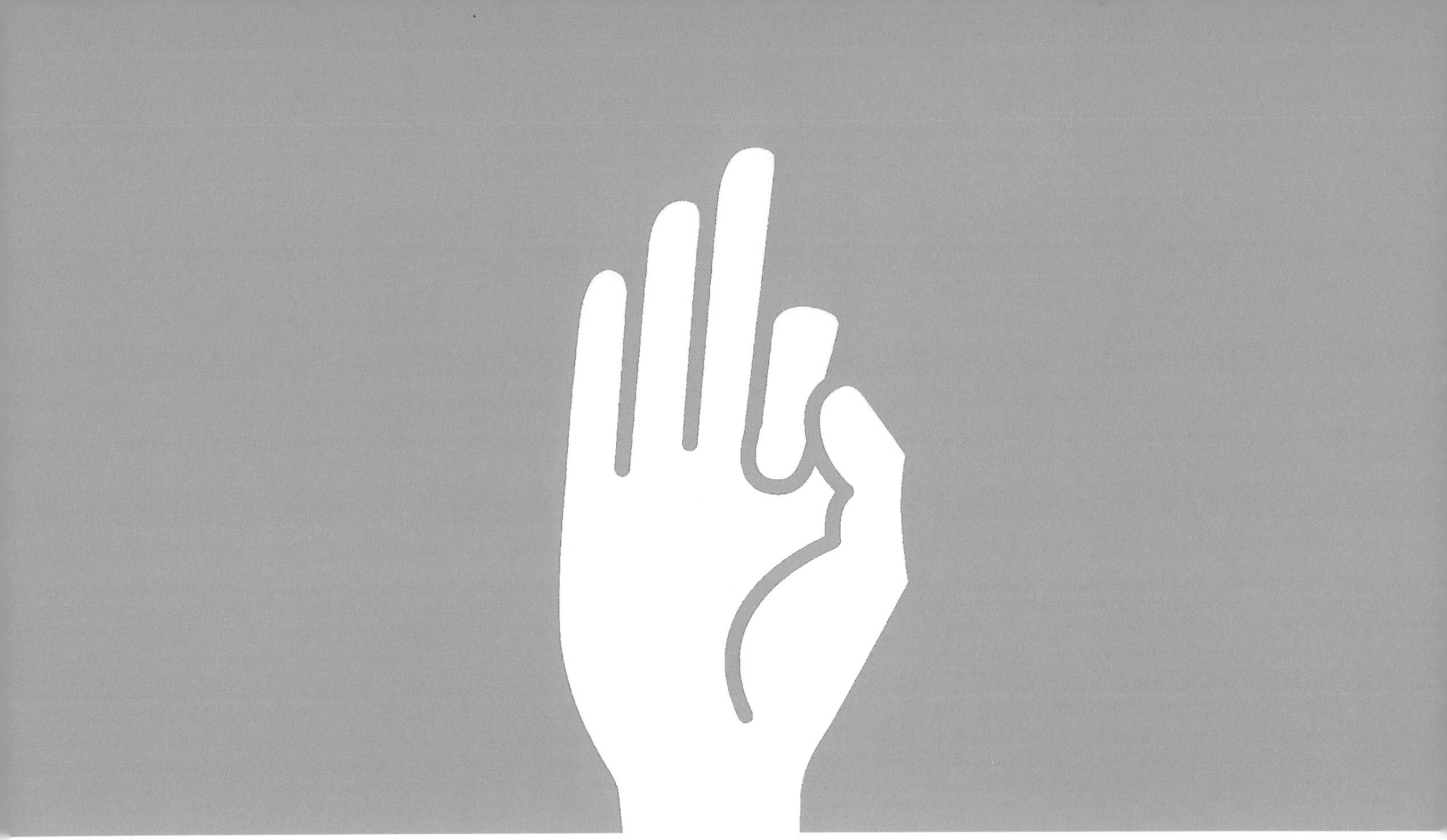

Ff

Gg

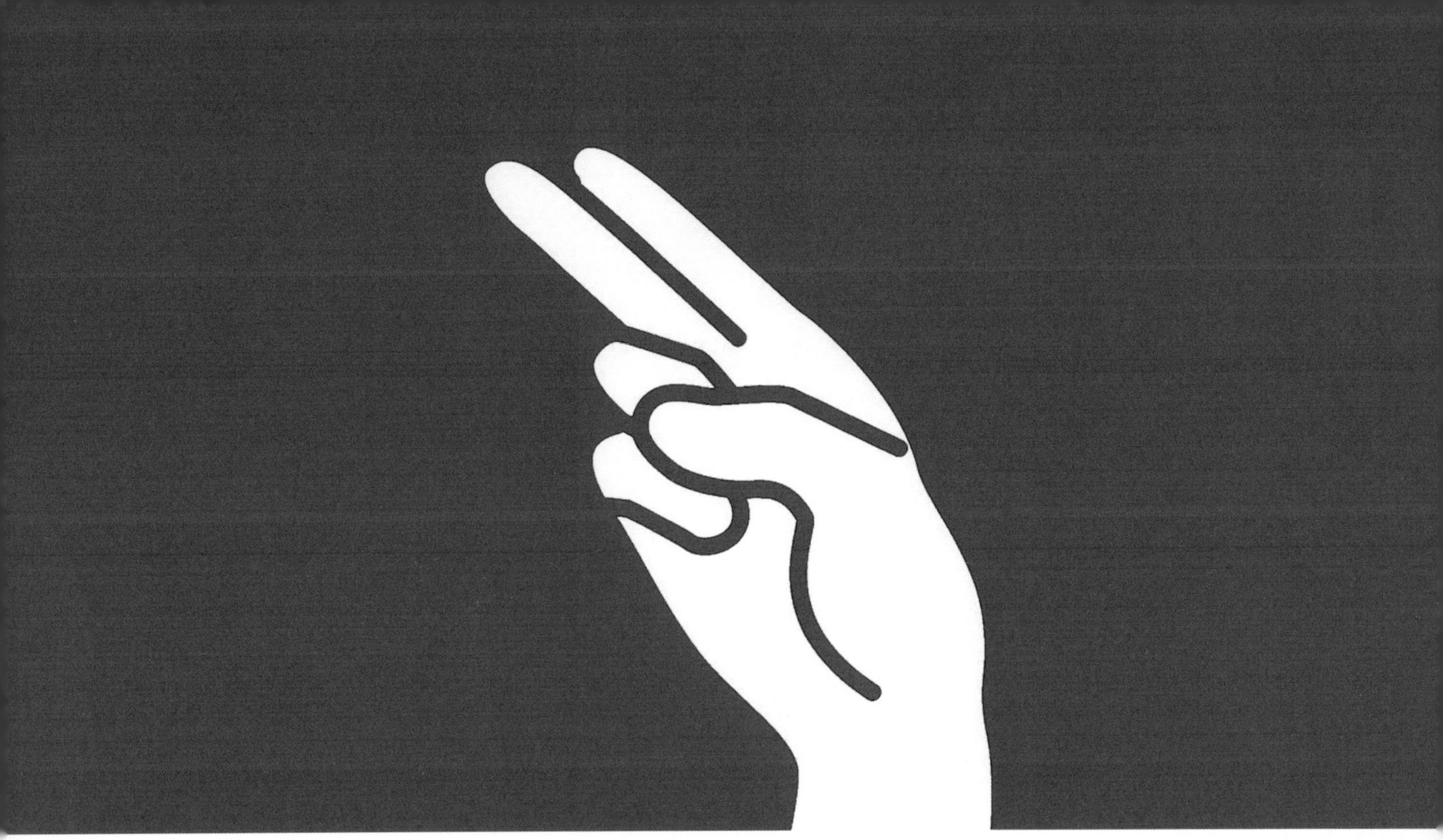

Hh

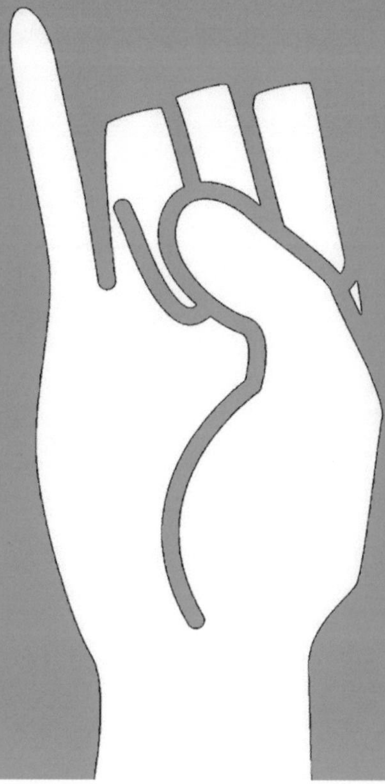

Ii

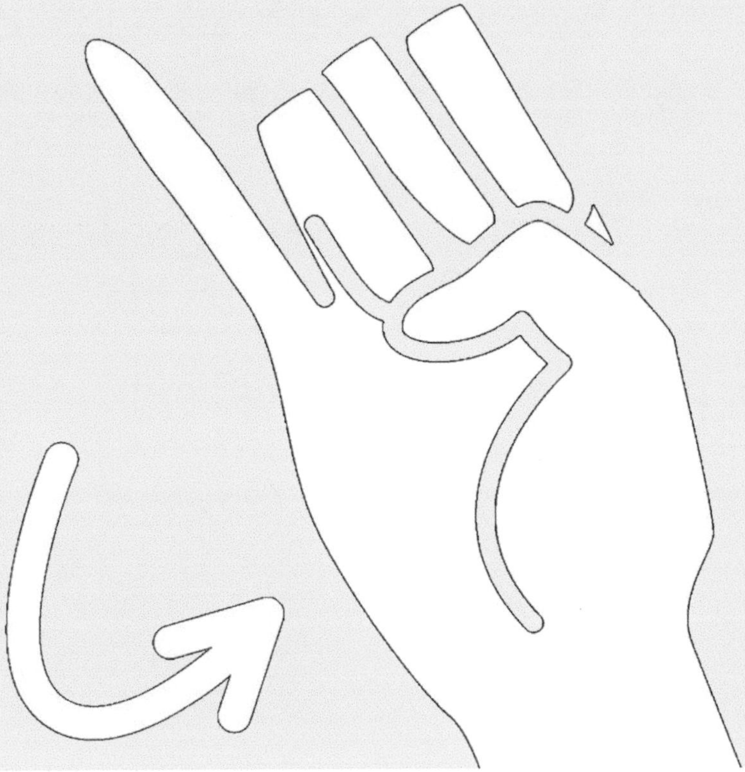

Jj

Kk

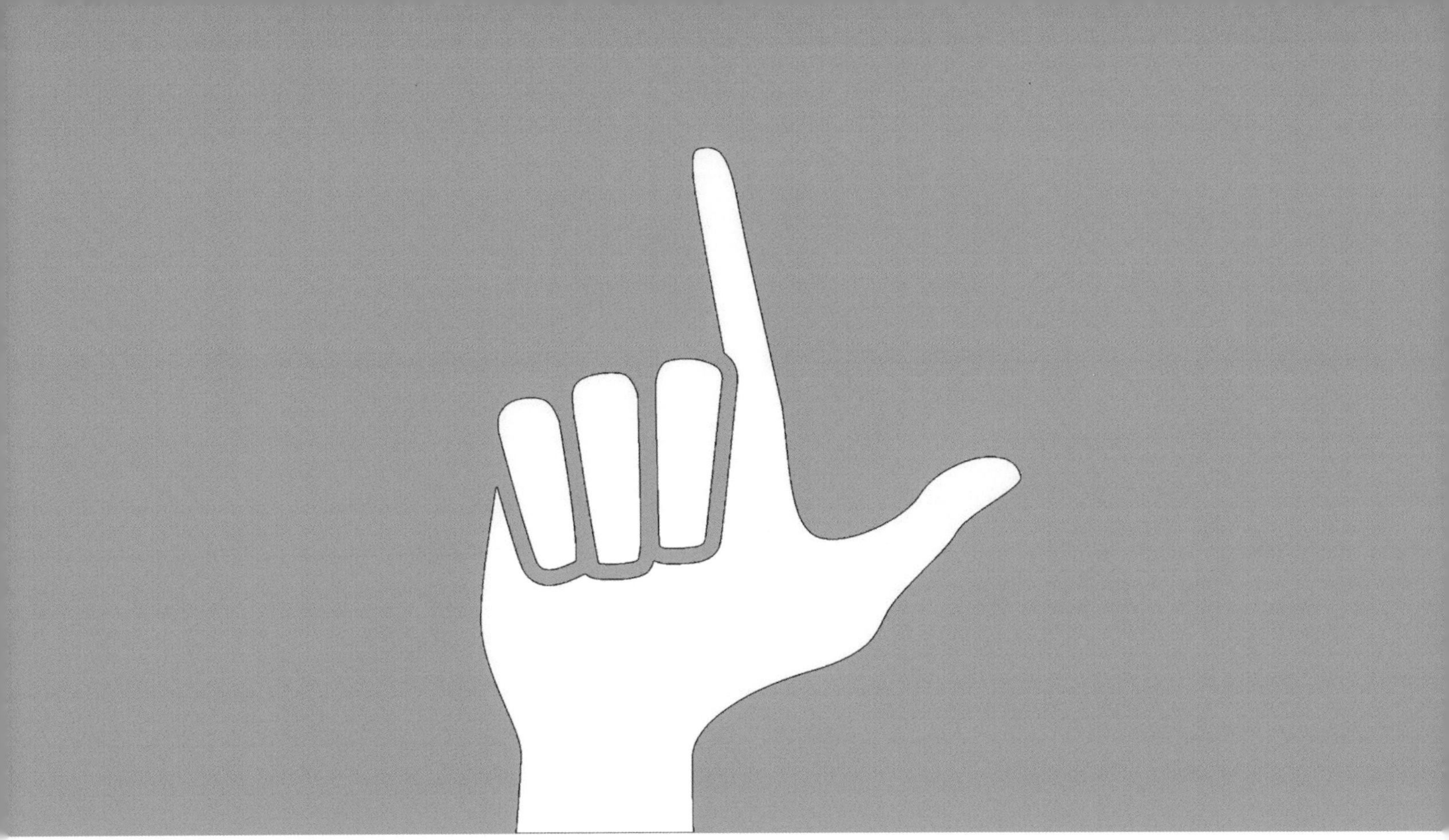

Ll

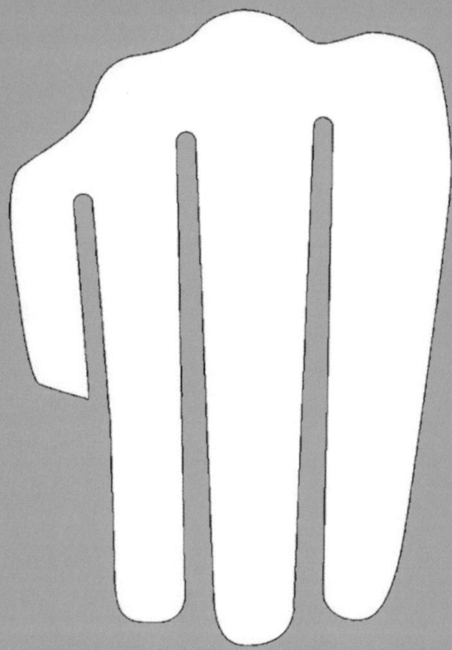

Mm

Nn

Oo

Pp

Qq

Rr

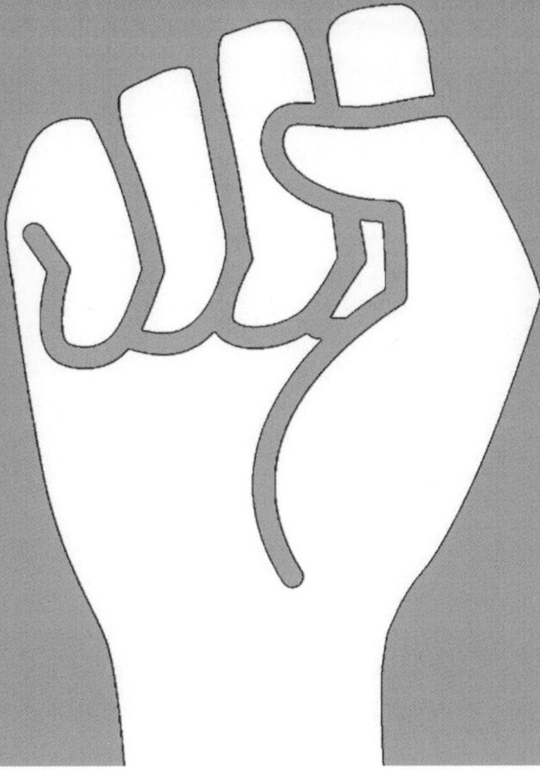

Ss

Tt

Uu

Vv

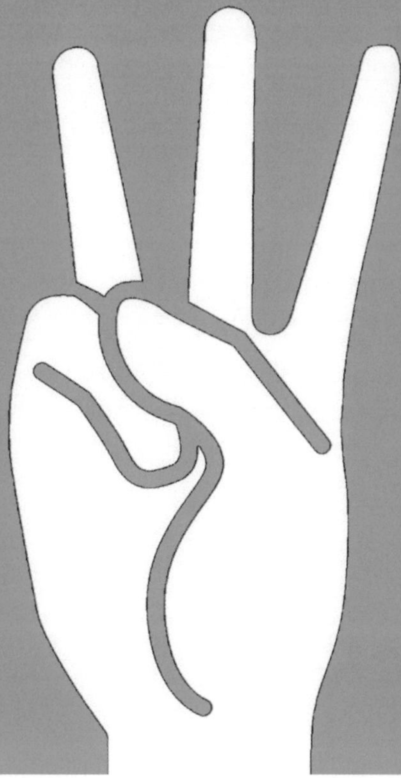

Ww

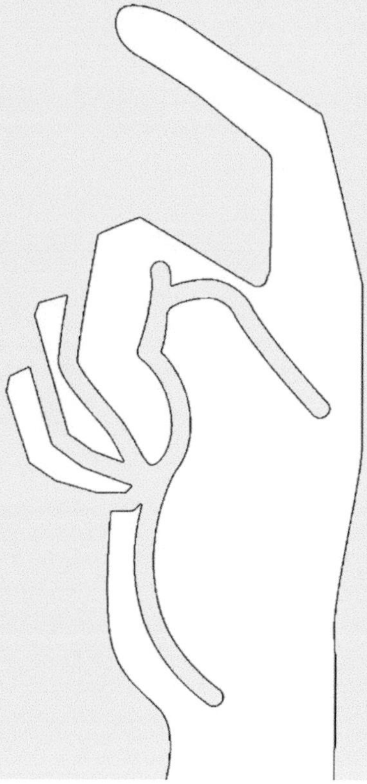

Xx

Yy

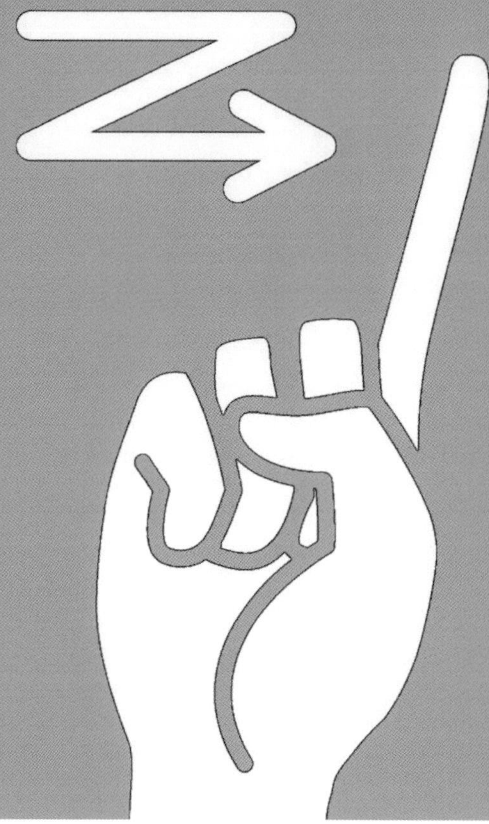

Zz

A B C D E F G
H I J K L M
N O P Q R S
T U V W X Y Z

Michael Terence
Publishing

Printed in Great Britain
by Amazon

14646786R00018